The American EAGLE
in Art and Design

321 Examples
Selected and Edited by
CLARENCE P. HORNUNG

Dover Publications, Inc.
New York

Dedicated to
Richard and Donald,
my two Eagle Scouts

FRONTISPIECE: Sculpture from the pedestal of the Lincoln Statue, Fort Wayne, Ind., by Paul Manship, 1931.

Published in Canada by General Publishing Company, Ltd., 30 Lesmill Road, Don Mills, Toronto, Ontario.
Published in the United Kingdom by Constable and Company, Ltd., 10 Orange Street, London WC2H 7EG.

The American Eagle in Art and Design: 321 Examples is a new work, first published by Dover Publications, Inc., in 1978.

DOVER *Pictorial Archive* SERIES

International Standard Book Number: 0-486-23604-8
Library of Congress Catalog Card Number: 77-15711

Manufactured in the United States of America
Dover Publications, Inc.
180 Varick Street
New York, N.Y. 10014

INTRODUCTION

When, in 1782, our founding fathers approved a "displayed" eagle (i.e., with outspread wings and legs) as a national seal, they could not have known what archeology has subsequently revealed—that 3000 years before Christ the eagle was the tutelary deity of Lagash in Mesopotamia, and was represented "displayed" in Babylonian cylinder seals with its head turned to the left, just as it is on our seal. The Chaldeans are thought to have been the first people to conceive of the high-flying eagle as a servant of the sun, and thus a symbol of immortality. For a long period the eagle, holding a thunderbolt or its prey, was a favorite emblem on the coinage of Greece and its colonial states. The eagle was represented on Roman coins, medals and gems playing its part in the apotheosis of the emperor, often with a palm branch in one claw. (During the ceremony it was customary that an eagle be released over the emperor's pyre to represent the soul ascending to heaven.) The spread eagle, grasping a thunderbolt in the talons of both claws, was encircled by a laurel wreath on the standards of the Roman legions. Double-headed eagles figured conspicuously as insignia of the Byzantine emperors and, beginning with Charlemagne (whose own device was the single-headed eagle of the legion, in the arms of the Holy Roman Empire. During the Middle Ages eagles, whether double- or single-headed, flourished as heraldic devices.

Thus the most probable explanation for the selection of the eagle as the national device is its association with classical antiquity. Since so many of the institutions of the new Republic were modeled on those of the old Roman Republic, and since this was the heyday of the Neoclassic revival in arts and letters, it was natural that the eagle of the Roman military standard, which had led the legions to victories on a thousand battlefields and which had been the emblem of the Caesars, with all its associations of majesty and power, prompted the choice of our emblem.

The first committee named by Congress to prepare a seal of the United States of America met on the afternoon of July 4, 1776, a few hours after the signing of the Declaration of Independence. Six years elapsed, one committee after another met and disbanded, one design after another was submitted, rejected or drastically revised, before arrival at the final choice, just five months before the signing of the peace treaty with Great Britain. Although other elements of the seal had appeared in earlier designs, the device submitted by William Barton of Philadelphia, who had been called in because of his knowledge of drawing and heraldry, was the first in which an eagle figured, "displayed" as "the Symbol of Supreme Power & Authority, [signifying] the Congress." After a second device, in which a small heraldic eagle was again displayed (in the crest), had been submitted by Barton, Congress ordered Charles Thomson, its Secretary, to take over. He eliminated the allegorical figures that had supported the shield on Barton's design, and made the eagle (not Barton's crested heraldic bird, but a bald-headed American eagle) the large central figure, bearing the shield on its breast and "in the dexter talons of the eagle an olive branch, and in the sinister a bundle of [thirteen] arrows." (Barton's original eagle had grasped a sword and a flag.) Over the head of the Thomson eagle was a constellation of thirteen stars, and in its beak was a scroll with the motto "E Pluribus Unum," the sole surviving feature of the design that had been submitted by the first committee in 1776. Thomson's device was given to Barton and, as redrawn by him with certain significant changes, was adopted on June 20, 1782 and later by the Federal Convention at Philadelphia in 1787. It was put in force by Washington's inauguration in 1789.

The die cut with the Great Seal was used until 1841, when Daniel Webster, the "Eagle of the East," was Secretary of State and the original die had become so worn that a new one was ordered to replace it. Hitherto the seal had been impressed over a white paper wafer which was affixed to the document with red wax. But about this time a new method of impressing the seal directly on the paper by means of a positive and negative die had come into use, and it was decided that the new seal should be cut to operate in this fashion. The work was entrusted to a Maryland engraver who seems to have been left entirely to his own devices. There were two signal errors in this second die: the equality of the pales was destroyed by making the red ones twice the width of the white, and the number of arrows in the eagle's claw was reduced from thirteen to six. Strangely enough, these mistakes passed unnoticed for many years. The seal was obviously illegal for, as Galliard Hunt points out in the *History of the Seal of the United States,* "unquestionably the Secretary of State has no authority to change the device of the arms, as it is prescribed by law, in the slightest degree, nor could the President himself properly authorize such a change. As the Seal was created by Congress it would require an Act of Congress to alter it."

In 1884, at the request of Theodore F. Frelinghuysen, Secretary of State, Congress appropriated $1000 to prepare a third die that would meet all hostile criticism raised against the illegal seal. After consulting various eminent authorities to consider the subject from the standpoints of history, heraldry and art, a new seal was designed by James Horton Whitehouse, chief designer for Tiffany & Co. This seal, bearing the design now in use, was cut in 1885. Bailey, Banks and Biddle of Philadelphia cut a precise copy in 1902.

After the adoption of the Great Seal, eagles, sometimes conforming closely to the original, but also in a wide variety of other postures and arrangements, promptly made their appearance on other official seals and insignia, notably those of different departments of the Federal Government, on the President's seal, on the seals of various states and on coins. Not infrequently, as in the President's seal, the eagle, for some unknown reason, turns its head towards its left instead of toward its right, which is correct. Some critics regard deviations, such as placing the arrows in the right claw and the olive branch in the left, reducing the number of arrows or of the pales in the shield, placing the eagle on the shield instead of the shield on the eagle, as being artistic liberties; others condemn them as being neither in conformity with heraldic

The first Great Seal, 1782.

law nor as prescribed by national law.

The eagle of the Great Seal, it should be noted, was not the first emblematic eagle to make its appearance in the American colonies. As early as 1700 an eagle had been stamped on a New York token of lead or brass; in 1776 it appeared on a Massachusetts copper penny in a semicircle of thirteen stars (before they spangled our banner); in 1778 the eagle perched on a globe in the arms of the State of New York. The eagle of the Great Seal is, however, the first to be designated as the American bald-headed species, distinguished from all others by its white head and tail. (Bald is here used in its other sense, meaning white.)

The eagle designed by Major Pierre Charles L'Enfant in 1784 as a badge for the Society of the Cincinnati was also specifically designated as the bald eagle. On seeing the badge, Benjamin Franklin wrote to his daughter from France

> I am, on this account not displeased that the figure is not known as a bald eagle but looks more like a turkey. For a truth, the turkey is in comparison a much more respectable bird and withal a true original native of America. Eagles have been found in all countries, but the turkey was peculiar to ours . . . He is, besides (though a little vain and silly, it is true, but not the worse emblem for that) a bird of courage, and would not hesitate to attack a grenadier of the British guards, who would presume to invade his farmyard with a *red* coat on.

He also expressed the wish

> that the bald eagle had not been chosen as the representative of our country; he is a bird of bad moral character; he does not get his living

The second Great Seal, 1841.

The present Great Seal.

honestly . . . too lazy to fish for himself, he watches the labor of the fishinghawk, and, when that diligent bird has at length taken a fish, and is bearing it to his nest for the support of his mate and young ones, the bald eagle pursues him and takes it from him. . . . like those among men who live by sharping and robbing he is generally poor, and often very lousy. Besides he is a rank coward; the little *kingbird,* not bigger than a sparrow, attacks him boldly and drives him out of the district.

In *The American Eagle, A Study in Natural and Civil History,* Francis Hobart Herrick comes stoutly to the defense of our national bird, clearing him of Franklin's charges and suggesting that they may have been inspired by pique because Franklin's design for the seal had been rejected when he was the chairman of the first committee. Herrick describes our bald-headed eagle as a native who has never been known to leave the continent of his own volition, who nests as near the sun as he can get, "like a true bird of Jove and messenger of the star of day," and as a model parent, devoting six months or more to rearing and training his young. Herrick also refutes Franklin's other charges: the bird is not a scavenger by any means, and is notable for its courage. He adds that if our eagle had possessed the brains of the dodo, he would have been virtually extinct by the end of the 18th century or the beginning of the 19th.

Despite Dr. Franklin's objections, the eagle soared into popular favor in 1789. When Washington made a triumphal tour of the thirteen states after his inauguration, eagles, traced on starched and whitewashed window panes illuminated by candles, shone in greeting. At balls in the President's honor fans and ribbons displayed eagles, and men's coat buttons had them engraved on them (as had the coat Washington wore during the inauguration ceremony). In a few years the eagle became probably the most popular motif in the decorative arts of this country; it would be difficult to think of an article or a medium that has not at one time or another borne our triumphant emblem. During the War of 1812, when patriotic fervor expressed itself in the arts and crafts as never before, the eagle's head with thirteen stars was even used to pattern a girl's wedding lace. And after the war had been won, craftsmen proudly reaffirmed the young Republic's freedom and power by working the bird into designs of every conceivable description. And a new brood of eagles has been brought forth for every subsequent war, Presidential campaign, exposition, fair and patriotic gathering.

With proper democratic impartiality, the eagle lent itself to the decoration of dinner porcelain and of kitchen crockery; it was mold-blown into whiskey flasks and pressed into Sandwich-glass cup plates; it winged its way over curtain and upholstery fabrics; it perched on mirrors, clocks and weather vanes as a finial; it was boldly carved into butter stamps and delicately inlaid in drawing-room furniture; it was painted on tavern signs and cast into flatiron holders; it was even stitched, star-surrounded, in finest needlework on quilted counterpanes, complete with arrows, olive branch and scroll.

It has been said that the mint breed of eagles has as many varieties and subspecies as dogs.

Often these eagles have been criticized as being of an alien breed, and for wearing the long feathered trousers that belong to the golden or international eagle. (The American eagle, except in its juvenal stage, has bare or half-bare shanks, extremely conspicuous because they are bright yellow.) But the eagle's adaptability in numismatics cannot compare with the mutations to which it has been subjected in objects of household use and decoration, in shop signs, in trademarks and printed ephemera. For most of the 19th century it was a favorite embellishment for stoneware crocks, jars, butter churns and water coolers, the earlier examples being small and crisply incised; the later ones large and brushed on in cobalt blue with bold calligraphic strokes or molded in relief. Pennsylvania-German potters sometimes incised it in their sgraffito pie plates in celebration of Presidential candidates. Some of the most handsome stylized eagles appear on humble Pennsylvania-German butter stamps carved by anonymous folk artists (usually in intaglio) in poplar, pine, walnut and the various fruit woods, as well as sugar maple, holly, birch and beech. One of these butter-stamp eagles would have gratified Franklin since its long legs make it look much more like a turkey than an eagle.

The spirited and beautiful eagles introduced in countless imaginative arrangements into pieced, knotted and other types of quilts testify not only to the skilled craftsmanship, but even more to the artistic invention of many generations of American women. The weavers also put eagles into the borders of their woven coverlets. Commemorative textiles of all kinds—mourning kerchiefs and those designed for other events (including those made to commemorate the Mexican War, the Philadelphia Centennial and Benjamin Harrison's inauguration in 1889) frequently incorporated eagles and shields in their designs along with portrait busts and battle scenes.

The most interesting and beautiful of our eagles are those which were carved in wood, either in relief or in the round, as decorative panels for sofas, chairs and mantelpieces, or to be placed over doorways, on cupolas and gate arches, as shop or tavern signs or as ships' figureheads. This medium—mahogany and pine were the preferred woods—attracted both self-taught folk artists (some of outstanding originality, such as the Pennsylvania German Wilhelm Schimmel, who worked with his disciple Aaron Mounts in the tradition of German peasant art in the post-Civil War years) and trained sculptors, architects and cabinetmakers of national reputation. One of the most distinguished was our first native-born sculptor, William Rush (1756–1833) among whose surviving works are two magnificent eagles carved as emblems, one for a church and the other for a fire company. Samuel McIntire, born a year after Rush, has been called "the most celebrated of the craftsmen-architects of America." He was fond of making an eagle in cameo-like relief the central motif of his exquisite mantels and of the cresting rails of his no less exquisite mahogany sofas, against a characteristic star-punched background. He also made eagles in the round, with closed wings, perched on globes, as ornaments for gate arches and cupolas. A noble spread eagle which once surmounted the door of the Old Custom House in his native Salem was his handiwork. His New York contemporary, Duncan Phyfe, like other cabinetmakers of the period, made charming mahogany chairs with eagle splats for distinguished clients.

Outstanding among these artist-craftsmen is John Haley Bellamy of Kittery Point, Maine, who devoted most of his long life (1836–1914) to eagles. He found his chief employment with the United States Government and with the Boston and Portsmouth Navy Yards, but he also made ornamental eagles for public and private buildings, and turned out innumerable highly distinctive eagles which may have been intended to hang over the doorways of ships' cabins. In order to symbolize the authority of the Federal Government, he developed a special technique for stylizing his fierce-beaked birds, which are extremely proud and graceful. They are usually brilliantly painted and gilded.

While the traditional thirteen stars frequently encircle the eagle in all media, sometimes the craftsman would introduce a purely decorative constellation, without regard to number. Especially in the case of marquetry eagles adorning fine mahogany, satinwood and maple chests of drawers, slant-top and tambour desks, secretaries, tall clocks, knife boxes and tip-top tables, the number of stars is that of the number of states of the Union at the time, which helps to date the pieces. Those with sixteen stars predominate and could have been made as early as 1796, when Tennessee was admitted, or as late as 1802, the year before Ohio came in, but probably were produced about 1798 (a year when diplomatic difficulties and a war of brief duration with France set off great political excitement). Marquetry eagles accompanied by eighteen stars

(Louisiana was admitted in 1812; Indiana in 1816) are further evidence of the intense nationalistic feeling roused by the War of 1812.

Cast-iron eagles are probably as numerous and diversified in character as those carved in wood, ranging from a tiny, delicately molded pin tray and a mechanical bank of an eagle feeding its young to a sign depicting a majestic creature with a wingspread of 65 inches soaring over the storm clouds. Some cast-iron eagles fall into odd categories that have become obsolete: wall anchors, snow catchers (placed at the edge of a roof to keep the snow from sliding off), stove urn finials (decorative humidifiers), stove plates and flatiron holders. Sometimes these eagles appear to derive from European prototypes and to have been adapted by tradition-loving craftsmen to new uses in a new land. Other metals have been used to make eagles: sheet copper was hammered into eagle weather vanes; the ventilating holes of the tin Pennsylvania food safes were sometimes pricked with eagle patterns; the eagle finials of grandfather clocks were of brass.

Other lands also used our emblem in their arts and crafts on works exported to the United States. It appeared in the cottons of the famous Oberkampf firm at Jouy, printed from the allegorical designs of contemporary artists. After Washington's death transfer-printed pottery jugs and punch bowls, made in Liverpool, featured our first President's tomb surrounded by weeping willows and grieving figures, among which an eagle mourns with drooping head. Most striking of these European creations is the Aubusson carpet in the drawing room of Mount Vernon, presented to Washington by Louis XVI, into which is woven an accurate representation of the Great Seal. The eagle of the Great Seal and the eagle of the Society of the Cincinnati were even enameled in far-off China, from American designs, on tea and dinner services, and were brought home in the holds of the clipper ships. Washington owned a complete dinner service and tea set of this Sino-Lowestoft porcelain with the insignia of the Cincinnati.

During the first two decades of the 20th century, renditions of the American eagle exhibited a carry-over from the academicism of the previous era. A strongly realistic treatment is seen in the bird's form, feathers and attitudes. Magazine covers of the period and World War I posters featured the conventional portrayal of the eagle; there was no deviation from the accepted forms. Following the war there was a tendency to experiment and stylistic changes began to appear, especially in the work of the graphic artists on trade and periodical covers as well as on other printed matter. (Greater latitude is open to the designer of the printed page; he is not as rigidly confined as is the artist whose medium is stone or bronze.) Examples of this wide variety of treatments may be seen in the group drawings executed by leading designers as chapter decorations for Merle Armitage's book *Accent on America.* They range from the conventional, naturalistic approach to free forms in which pure geometrical design dominates the bird's structure and details.

The postwar period witnessed fundamental changes in sculptural expression influenced by the enormous development in abstract art, here and abroad. The first quarter of the century saw the birth of cubism, futurism and many other revolutionary movements. Symbols of this rupture with tradition, while not nearly as extreme as is to be found in the field of painting, nevertheless are manifest in the work of many sculptors whose

The eagle continues as a powerful symbol of the United States. Edward Grove created this plaster model for the monument that Palm Beach, Florida, dedicated on July 4, 1976 to commemorate the American Bicentennial.

roots were firmly planted in the past. Sculptors, modelers and medalists with academic training loosened their bonds with the past when exposed to modern influences. Such giants as Lee Lawrie, Paul Manship, Adolph Weinman, Paul Jennewein, Donald De Lue, George Lober, Cesare Gaetano and a host of others, working on important government commissions for post offices, courthouses and war memorials reached their fullest maturity with the creation of vigorous sculptures distinguished both in composition and in detail. The wide range of their differing techniques and personalized interpretations affords an interesting study.

These changes in the portrayal of the eagle from one period to the next serve but to strengthen and make more viable our national emblem. Whatever trends may lie ahead, the American eagle, a symbol of our unity, purpose and fortitude, will continue to gather strength.

CLARENCE P. HORNUNG

BIBLIOGRAPHY

Bingham, R. W., "George Washington in Lowestoft Ware"; *Antiques,* July, 1927.

Cigrand, B. J., "Story of the Great Seal of the United States."

Earle, Alice Morse, *China Collecting in America;* Charles E. Tuttle, Rutland, Vermont, 1971 (reprint).

Halsey, R. T. H., *Homes of Our Ancestors.*

Herrick, Francis Hobart, *The American Eagle, A Study in Natural and Civil History;* D. Appleton-Century Company, Incorporated, New York, 1934.

Hodgson, James, American Flags, Seals and Insignia.

Homes, H. A., The Correct Arms of the State of New York, as established by law since March 16, 1778.

Hornung, Clarence P., *Treasury of American Design* (2 vols.); Harry N. Abrams, New York, 1972.

Hunt, Galliard, *The History of the Seal of the United States;* U.S. Printing Office, Washington, 1909.

Isaacson, Philip M., *The American Eagle;* New York Graphic Society, Boston, 1975.

Keyes, Homer Eaton, "American Eagle Lowestoft"; *Antiques,* June, 1930.

————, "The Cincinnati and Their Porcelain"; *Antiques,* February, 1930.

Kimball, Fiske, *Mr. Samuel McIntire, Carver, the Architect of Salem;* Essex Institute of Salem, Salem, 1940.

————, "Furniture Carvings by Samuel McIntire"; *Antiques,* December, 1930.

Marceau, Henri, *William Rush, 1756-1833, The First Native American Sculptor;* Pennsylvania Museum of Art, Philadelphia, 1937.

Mercer, H. C., *The Bible in Iron;* Bucks County Historical Society, Doylestown, Pennsylvania, 1961.

Metropolitan Museum of Art, *Handbook of the American Wing.*

Museum of Modern Art, *American Folk Art: The Art of the Common Man in America, 1750–1900;* Arno Press, New York, 1970 (reprint).

Newark Museum Association, *American Folk Sculpture;* 1932.

————, *New English Dictionary on Historical Principles,* 1919.

Safford, Victor, "John Haley Bellamy, The Wood Carver of Kittery Point"; *Antiques,* March, 1935.

Thomas, Stephen W., "Major Samuel Shaw and the Cincinnati Porcelain"; *Antiques,* May, 1935.

Tiemann, Bernard J., "The Symbols of the U.S.A. and its Possessions"; unpublished manuscript, The Numismatic Society, 1923.

Zieker, Eugene, *Heraldry in America;* Haskell House Publications, Inc., New York, 1969 (reprint).

The American EAGLE
in Art and Design

1. By Arthur H. Fisher, Washington Zoo, 1940.

2. By Arthur H. Fisher, Washington Zoo, 1940. 3. By Margaret Bourke-White, the New York Zoological Garden, 1940.

4. By Arthur H. Fisher, Washington Zoo, 1940.

5. By Arthur H. Fisher, Washington Zoo, 1940.

6–8. By Arthur H. Fisher, Washington Zoo, 1940.

9. By Arthur H. Fisher, Washington Zoo, 1940.

10

11

10, 11. By Arthur H. Fisher, Washington Zoo, 1940.

12. Lithograph by Edward Lear.

13. Engraving by John James Audubon in *The Birds of America*, 1840. 14. Engraving by Alexander Wilson from *American Ornithology*, 1808–14.

35, 36. Typographic eagles from 19th-century typefounders' specimen catalogues.

37, 38. Typographic eagles from 19th-century typefounders' specimen catalogues.

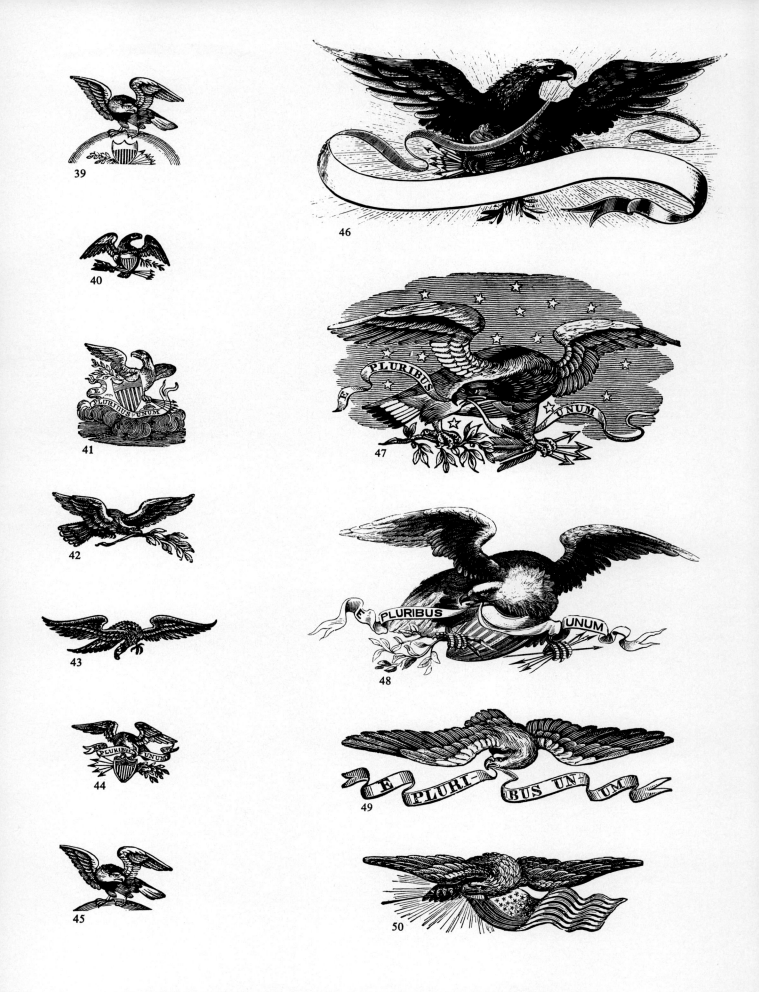

39–50. Typographic eagles from 19th-century typefounders' specimen catalogues.

51–58. Typographic eagles from 19th-century typefounders' specimen catalogues.

NATHANIEL C. KNAPP,   LEVI RIGHTMYER.

59

LIBERTY AND UNION. ONE AND INSEPARABLE.

60

59, 60. 19th-century calligraphic eagles from penmanship manuals.

61–63. 19th-century calligraphic eagles from penmanship manuals.

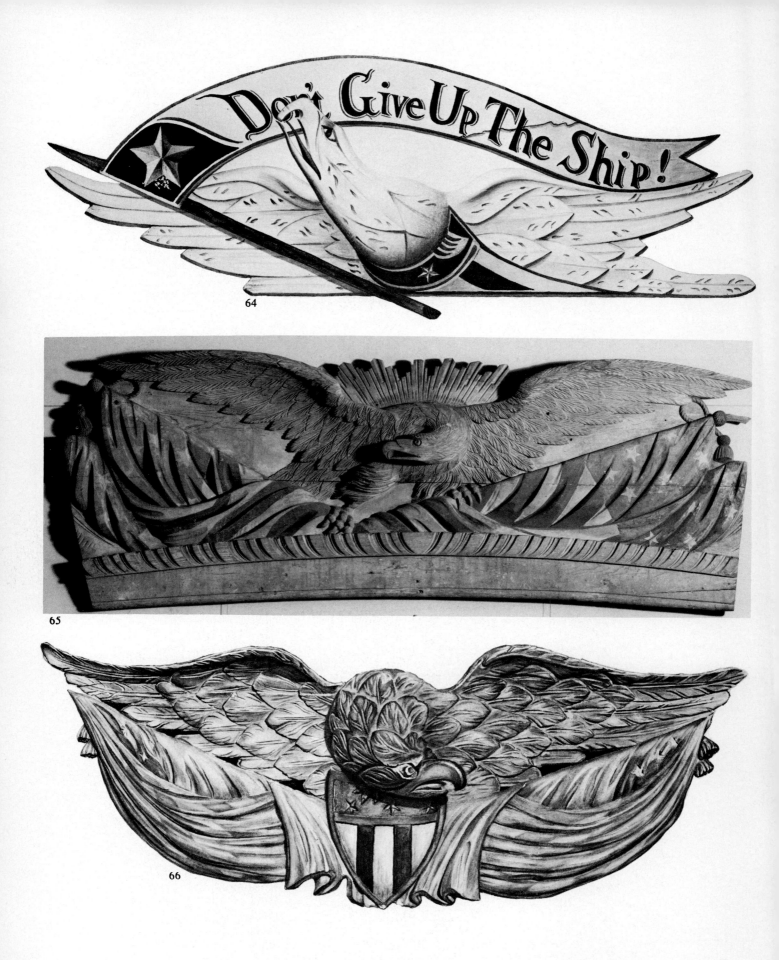

64. Late 19th-century wooden ship decoration by John Bellamy. **65.** Late 19th-century sternboard decoration. **66.** Wooden sternboard decoration by John Bellamy, Maine, 1850–80.

67. Late 19th-century sternpiece decoration. **68.** Sternpiece for the *Rousseau*, mid-19th century. **69.** Figurehead for S.S. *Lancaster*, by John Bellamy, 1880.

70. Mahogany eagle, early 19th century. **71.** 19th-century polychrome eagle.

72. Mid 19th-century eagle showing Napoleonic influences. **73, 74.** Eagle attributed to Samuel McIntire, 1804.

75. Pine billethead from the *Great Republic,* by Samuel W. or William Gleason, 1854. **76.** Late 19th-century billethead. **77.** Pine billethead, 1850.

78. Late 19th-century billethead. **79, 80.** Mid 19th-century billethead.

81. Eagle by William Rush, c. 1808, from Independence Hall. 82. Mantel decoration by Samuel McIntire, 1806. 83. Wooden eagle. 84. Painted pine eagle by William Rush, c. 1810. 85. c. 1830.

83

84

85

86   87

88   89

86–89. 19th-century butter molds. **90, 92.** Eagles attributed to Wilhelm Schimmel, 1865–90.
91. Eagle mottled black and yellow, mid 19th century.

90

91

92

93

94

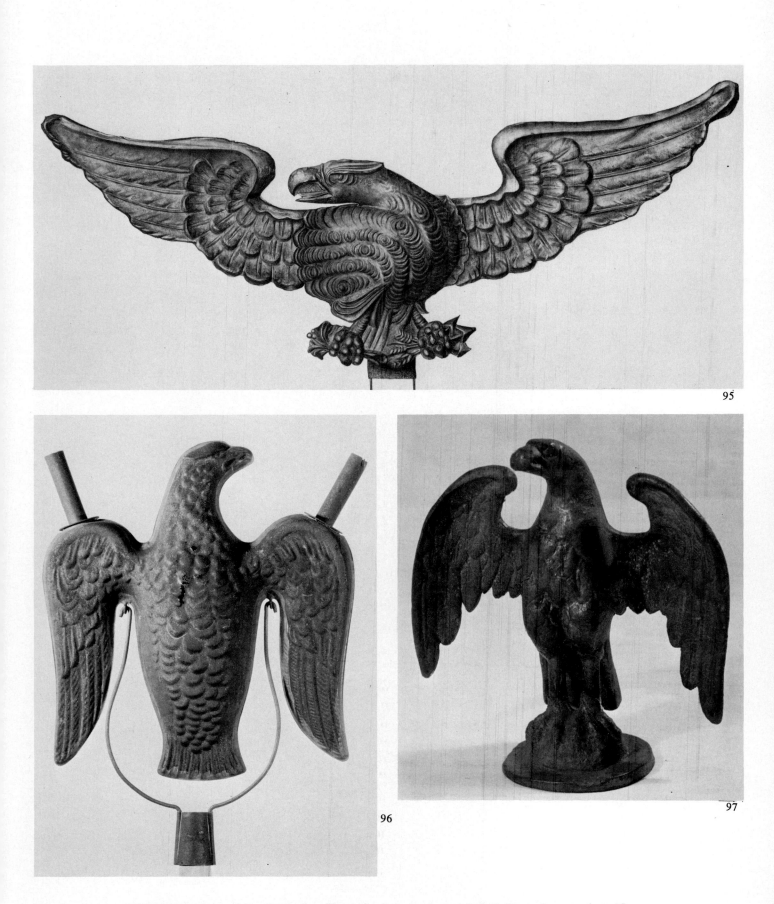

95

96

97

93. Brass eagle used as decoration for reviewing stand at Admiral Dewey's reception, New York, 1899. 94. Stamped sheet-zinc weather vane, c. 1875. 95. Stamped brass decoration for reviewing stand, 1840–50. 96. Torchère of stamped tin. 97. Lead eagle.

98

99

98. Polychrome cast-iron eagle. **99.** Cast-iron gatepost finial.

100. Cast-iron grille, c. 1840. **101.** Cast-iron building decoration, c. 1850.

102. Copper finial. **103.** Sheet-copper weather vane.

104. Sheet-copper and cast-lead weather vane, early 19th century. **105.** Gilded weather vane of molded copper.

106. Metal eagle. **107.** Urn with metal eagle as finial on lid. **108.** Cast-iron snowcatcher.

109. Cast-brass door knocker.

110

111

110. Flag with painted eagle. c. 1781. **111.** Appliqué coverlet of cotton goods, c. 1850. **112.** Early 19th-century English printed cotton. **113.** Printed cotton kerchief commemorating the War of 1812, c. 1815. **114.** Handmade hooked rug of homespun wool, c. 1800.

112

113

114

115

115. Wool-and-cotton coverlet with the Great Seal, 1831. **116.** Coverlet, 1832. **117.** Woven coverlet, 1845. **118.** Coverlet, 1846. **119.** Coverlet.

116 118

117

119

120

121

122

120. Ceramic pitcher by Tucker & Hemphill, Philadelphia, c. 1835. **121.** Cup plate by John Rogers & Son, Staffordshire, England, 1815–42. **122.** Early 19th-century Staffordshire cup plate. **123.** Mid 19th-century ceramic statuette. **124.** Glass mug commemorating the entrance of Vermont into the Union, 1791.

123

124

133, 135. World War I posters by Charles Livingston Bull. 134. World War II poster by Tom Woodburn. 136. World War I poster by James H. Daugherty.

THE SHIPS
ARE COMING

UNITED STATES SHIPPING BOARD   EMERGENCY FLEET CORPORATION

137, 138, 140. Covers by Clarence P. Hornung. **139.** Paper-sculpture cover.

141. Cover by Walt Harris. **142–144.** Covers by Robert Foster.

145

I PLEDGE ALLEGIANCE TO THE FLAG
OF THE UNITED STATES OF AMERICA,
AND TO THE REPUBLIC FOR WHICH
IT STANDS; ONE NATION, INDIVISIBLE,
WITH LIBERTY AND JUSTICE FOR ALL.

E PLURIBUS UNUM

UNITED WE STAND

146

An American's
CALENDAR
·1942·

Designed by Clarence Pearson Hornung

145–147. Patriotic designs by Clarence P. Hornung, 1942–50.

148–153. Trademarks and emblems by Clarence P. Hornung.

154–157. Trademarks and emblems by Clarence P. Hornung. **158.** Trademark by Raymond Loewy & Associates.

1943 1944

159

BOOKS ARE WEAPONS IN THE WAR OF IDEAS

160

OUR MEN WANT
★ BOOKS ★

SEND
ALL YOU CAN SPARE ★
ASK YOUR BOOKSELLER HOW 161

SAVE WHEAT SAVE MEAT

SAVE THE PEACE

162

159–162. Drawings by Clarence P. Hornung, 1942–47.

Illustrations. **163.** By Clarence P. Hornung. **164.** By Merle Armitage. **165.** By Paul Landacre.
166. By Maynard Dixon. **167.** By Eugen Maier-Krieg.

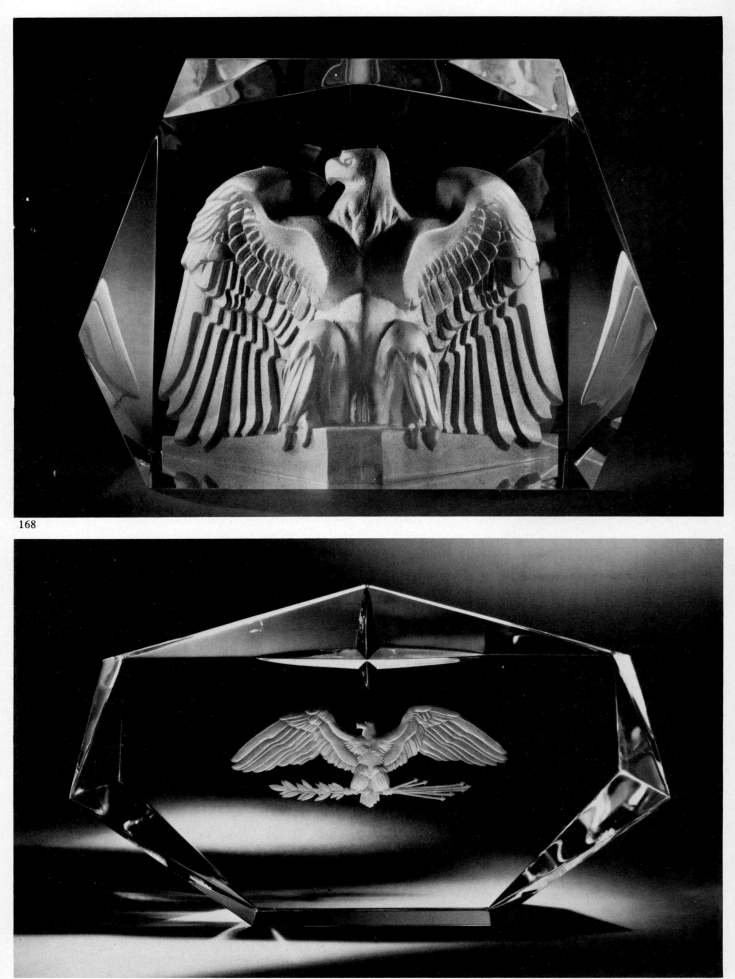

168

169

170

Designs for Steuben Glass, **168.** Faceted crystal by Donald Pollard. **169.** Crystal plaque engraved by Sidney Waugh, designed by George Thompson. **170.** Bowl by Donald Pollard with engraving by Sidney Waugh.

174

175

Designs for Steuben Glass. **174.** Crystal eagle. **175.** Crystal bowl presented to Princess Beatrix of the Netherlands.

176

177

176. Crystal prism designed by James Houston for Steuben Glass. **177.** Plaster model by Carl Schnitz for glass bowl by Verlys.

178, 179. Gold eagles on crystal settings by James Houston for Steuben Glass.

Metal letter boxes. **180.** Old Merchants National Bank & Trust Co., Chicago. **181.** By Cutler Mail Chute Co., c. 1915. **182.** La Salle Building, Chicago, c. 1920. **183.** Chrysler Building, New York City, by Cutler Mail Chute Co., 1929.

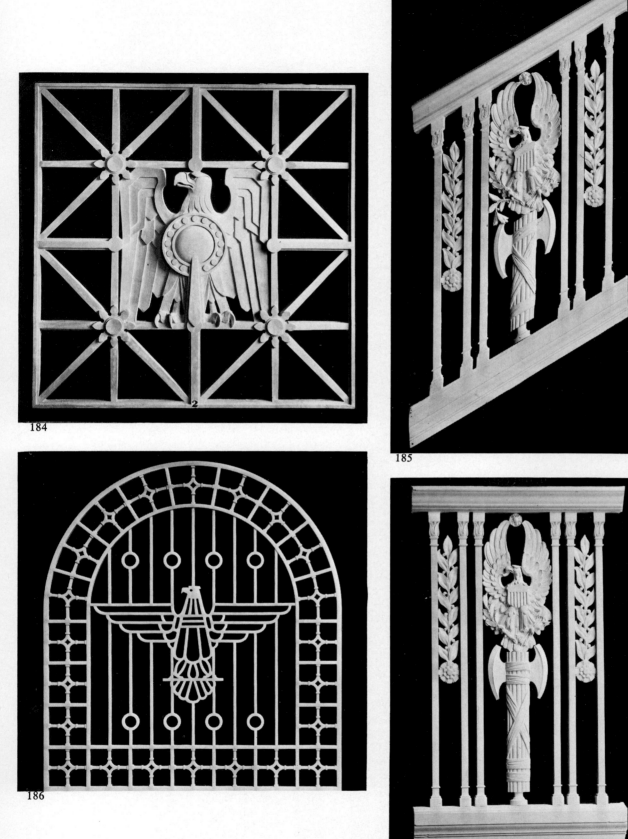

184. Model for metal grille for Bureau of Printing and Engraving Annex, by Lombard & Ludwig, 1936. **185.** Model for metal grille for post office, Stillwater, Okla., by Washington Ornamental Co., 1933. **186, 187.** Models for iron stair rails, Federal Office Building, Seattle, Wash., 1932.

188

189   190

Models for metal grilles. **188.** Office and Residence of the U.S. High Commissioner, Manila, by F. Bruyninck, 1938. **189.** Post office and courthouse, Savannah, Ga., by Lombard & Ludwig, 1931. **190.** Post office, Elgin, Tex., by Lombard & Ludwig, 1938.

191. Metal sculpture by Marshall Fredericks.

192

193

194

192–194. Metal sculptures by Robert Foster, 1930–39.

195. Model for pylon decoration, Ohio River Bridge, Louisville, Ky.

196

197

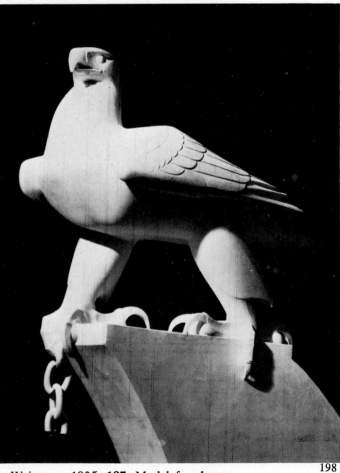

198

196. War Memorial, Pottstown, Pa., by Adolph A. Weinman, 1935. **197.** Model for decoration, memorial, Central Park, New York City, by Georg Lober. **198.** Model for Spanish-American War Monument, Rochester, N.Y., by C. Paul Jennewein, 1940.

199

200

199, 201. Models for granite decoration, Pennsylvania Station, New York City, by Adolph A. Weinman, c. 1910. **200, 202.** Models, tower of University of Chicago Chapel, by Ulric H. Ellerhusen.

201

202

203

204

203. Model, tower of University of Chicago Chapel, by Ulric H. Ellerhusen. **204.** Model for main entrance to Washington Hall, West Point, by Lee Lawrie.

205

206

205. Architectural eagle, 1935. **206.** Ornament for Federal Building, New York World's Fair, 1939, by Gifford Proctor.

207. Model for a statue by A. Stirling Calder. **208.** Model of sculpture for Memorial Monument, Tours, France, by C. Paul Jennewein, 1933. **209.** The finished sculpture in place.

210, 211. Details of model for pediment, United States Archives Building, Washington, D.C., by Adolph A. Weinman. **212.** Honolulu Memorial, by Bruce Moore.

210

211

212

213. Bronze memorial tablet, Consolidated Gas Co., New York City, 1932. **214.** Model submitted by Gaetano Cecere in design competition for the Tomb of the Unknown Soldier.

215. Model for Federal Reserve Building, Boston, by Donald De Lue. **216.** *Day,* relief on U.S. Post Office Department Building, Washington, D.C., by Anthony de Francisci.

217

218

217. Model for relief, Pennsylvania Station, New York City, by Adolph A. Weinman, c. 1910. **218.** Detail, Lincoln Memorial, Washington, D.C.

219. Model for post office, Schenectady, N.Y., by Anthony Di Lorenzo. **220.** Model for Hartford County Building, Hartford, Conn. **221.** Model for post office, Cape Charles, Va., by Silbermann & Matthew, 1932.

222

223

224

225

226

222. Model for pier head and corbel, West Point, by Lee Lawrie. **223.** Model for post office, Scranton, Pa., by Washington Ornamental Co., 1930. **224.** Model for Appraisers Stores and Immigration Station, San Francisco, by Lombard & Ludwig, 1940. **225.** Model for post office, Vinita, Okla., by Lombard & Ludwig, 1939. **226.** Model for Queens Borough Hall, New York City, by René Chambellan.

227

228

227. Model for post office, Gloversville, N.Y., by Enca Buford, 1936. **228.** Model for Englewood postal station, Chicago, 1938.

229. Model for post office, Poughkeepsie, N.Y., by Emil Jung, 1937.

230

231

230. Frieze on bird house, Central Park Zoo, New York City, by Siebern. **231.** Relief, Rockefeller Center, New York City, by Lee Lawrie, 1930s.

232. Model for courthouse, Philadelphia, by Donald De Lue. **233.** East Coast Memorial, New York City, by Albino Manca, 1960. **234.** Relief, Rockefeller Center, New York City, by Robert Garrison, 1930s.

235

236

237

235. Model for post office, Canoga Park, Cal., by Architectural Sculptors, 1939. **236.** Model for post office, Wenatchee, Wash., by Emil Jung, 1937. **237.** Model for post office, Hyannis, Mass., by Washington Ornamental Co., 1938.

238. Model for post office, Rahway, N.J., by Lombard & Ludwig, 1936. **239.** Model for American Embassy, Paris, by John Donnelly. **240.** Model for post office, West Frankfort, Ill., by Studio of Architectural Sculpture, 1935.

241. Model for Myron Taylor Memorial, Ithaca, N.Y., by Lee Lawrie, 1931. **242.** Model for Washington Hall, West Point, by Lee Lawrie.

243

244

243. Model for San Francisco Mint by Albert Stewart. **244.** Model for commemorative plaque, Jamaica Estates, N.Y., by John R. Terken.

245. Eagle over entrance to former Whitney Museum of Art, New York City. **246.** Model for post office, South Norwalk, Conn., by Gaetano Cecere. **247.** Model for panel, San Diego, Cal.

248

249

248. Model for fountain outlet, Julius Fleischman estate, Cincinnati, O., by Edmond R. Amateis. **249.** Model for post office, Altoona, Pa., by Frank Vittor, 1932.

250

251

250. Model for bronze decoration, post office and courthouse, Greenville, S.C., 1936. **251.** Model for pedimental figure, Illinois Merchant Bank, Chicago, by Henry Hering.

252. Model for post office, Astoria, Ore., by Bussard-Nelson Co., 1931. **253.** Model for bronze panel, Federal Reserve Bank, Cleveland, O., by Henry Hering. **254.** Bronze clock ornaments, Bank of the United States, New York City.

255

255. Model for spandrel, Arlington Memorial Bridge, Washington, D.C., by C. Paul Jennewein.
256. Model for post office, Greenville, Va., by Clepper & Clepper, 1933. **257.** Medallion,
Federal Trade Commission Building, Washington, D.C., by Sidney Waugh. **258.** Model for
post office, Littlefield, Tex., 1940.

256

257

258

259. Model for Social Security Building, Washington, D.C., by Richmond Barthe. **260.** Model for Federal Office Building, Helena, Mont., 1932. **261.** Model for Federal Office Building, Cheyenne, Wyo., 1933.

262. Model for President's Seal, Roosevelt Library, Hyde Park, New York, 1941. **263.** Model for post office, New Castle, Pa., by Frank Vittor, 1933. **264.** Model for courthouse, Fort Worth, Tex., by Anthony Di Lorenzo. **265.** Model for Federal Reserve Bank Building, Washington, D.C.

266. Model for post office, Flushing, N.Y., by Rochette and Parzini, 1933. **267.** Model for post office and courthouse, Columbus, O., by J. C. Lombard Company, 1933. **268.** Illustration from catalogue of United States Bronze Sign Company.

269

270

271

269. Decoration, courthouse, Brooklyn, New York. **270.** Model for National Cemetery, San Bruno, Cal., by F. Bruyninck, 1948. **271.** Model for Station "Y" post office, New York City, by Lombard & Ludwig, 1935.

272. Model for post office and courthouse, Los Angeles, by Lombard & Ludwig, 1938.
273. Model for the Oregon State Seal. **274.** Model for bronze plaque, Federal Reserve Building, Washington, D.C.

275. Model for Department of Justice Building, Washington, D.C., by C. Paul Jennewein.
276. Arms of the state of New York, Jones Beach Tower, New York, by Ulric Ellerhusen.
277. Arms of the state of New York, cast in aluminum, on Family Courts Building, New York City, by Harry Poole Camden.

278. $10 gold "eagle" (liberty-cap type), minted 1795–1804. **279.** Silver half dollar (bust type), 1794–1807. **280.** Dime (bust or Liberty type), 1796–1807. **281.** Silver quarter (turban-head type), 1815–38. **282.** Silver half dollar (turban-head type) 1807–39. **283.** Silver dollar (Liberty seated), 1840–73. **284.** Copper penny (flying-eagle type) 1856–58. **285.** Silver trade dollar (Liberty seated), 1873–85. **286.** Silver dollar (Morgan type), 1878–1921. **287.** $10 gold coin (coronet type), 1838–1907.

288. $5 gold coin (coronet type), 1840–1907. **289.** $10 gold coin (Indian-head type), designed by Augustus Saint-Gaudens, 1907–1933. **290.** $20 gold coin (Liberty-standing type) designed by Augustus Saint-Gaudens. **291.** $5 gold coin (Indian-head type), 1908–29. **292.** Silver half dollar (Liberty-walking type), designed by Adolph A. Weinman. **293.** $1 coin "(Peace" dollar), designed by Anthony de Francisci, 1922. **294.** Quarter (Liberty-standing type), designed by Hermon A. MacNeil, 1916. **295.** Half dollar (Kennedy type), 1964. **296.** Quarter (Washington type), designed by John Flanagan, 1932.

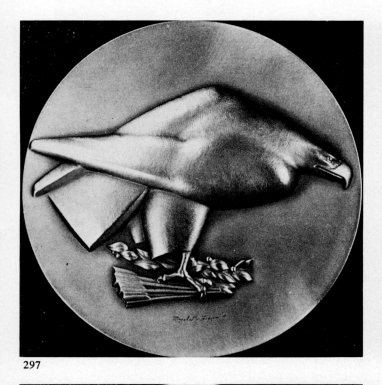

297. Eaton Manufacturing Company Eagle Medal by Marshall M. Fredericks, 1948. **298.** Model for George M. Cohan Congressional Gold Medal by Erwin Springweiler. **299.** Mathieson Alkali Works 50th Anniversary medal by René P. Chambellan, 1942. **300.** Model for Concord Art Association Medal by Albert Laessle.

301

302

303

304

301. American Institute of Architects medal by Adolph A. Weinman, 1907. **302.** Medal by Warner Williams, 1968. **303.** Association of Federal Architects medal, 1927. **304.** Collier's Magazine Award for Congressional Service, by Robert Foster, 1945.

305

306

307

308

305. Congressional Medal of Honor Society Medallion, 1968. **306.** Presidential Seal Medallion by Ralph J. Menconi, 1968. **307.** Henry Hering Memorial Medal by Albino Manca, 1959. **308.** 46th Issue, Society of Medalists by Karl Gruppe, 1952.

309   310

311   312

309. Presidential Seal by Sidney Waugh, 1951. **310.** American Legion 50th Anniversary Medal by C. Paul Jennewein, 1969. **311.** Philadelphia Bicentennial Medal by Frank Gasparro, 1976. **312.** Declaration of War Medallion, by Harvey Eli, 1917.

313

314

315   316

313. University of Iowa Distinguished Service Medallion by Anthony Notaro, 1963. **314.** Tennessee Technological University Seal Medal by Hans Ernst Prehn, 1965. **315.** Rebild National Park American Independence Day Medal by Marshall Fredericks, 1972. **316.** Catholic University of America 75th Anniversary Medal by Claire Fontanini, 1964.

317   318

319   320

317. Audubon Artists Creative Medal by Mario Cooper, 1961. **318.** Council of American Artist Societies Medal by Wheeler Williams, 1964. **319.** Indiana Bicentennial Series Patrick Henry Medal by Warner Williams, 1972. **320.** Elizabeth Sprague Coolidge Medal by Dora Clarke, 1932.